STEAM JOBS IN
Internet Technology

Carole Hawkins

Rourke
Educational Media

A Division of
Carson Dellosa
Education

rourkeeducationalmedia.com

Before Reading: *Building Background Knowledge and Vocabulary*

Building background knowledge can help children process new information and build upon what they already know. Before reading a book, it is important to tap into what children already know about the topic. This will help them develop their vocabulary and increase their reading comprehension.

Questions and Activities to Build Background Knowledge:

1. Look at the front cover of the book and read the title. What do you think this book will be about?
2. What do you already know about this topic?
3. Take a book walk and skim the pages. Look at the table of contents, photographs, captions, and bold words. Did these text features give you any information or predictions about what you will read in this book?

Vocabulary: *Vocabulary Is Key to Reading Comprehension*

Use the following directions to prompt a conversation about each word.

- Read the vocabulary words.
- What comes to mind when you see each word?
- What do you think each word means?

Vocabulary Words:
- algorithms
- cyberattacks
- hackers
- implement
- intact
- microchip
- remotely
- routers
- scrambled
- static

During Reading: *Reading for Meaning and Understanding*

To achieve deep comprehension of a book, children are encouraged to use close reading strategies. During reading, it is important to have children stop and make connections. These connections result in deeper analysis and understanding of a book.

 Close Reading a Text

During reading, have children stop and talk about the following:

- Any confusing parts
- Any unknown words
- Text to text, text to self, text to world connections
- The main idea in each chapter or heading

Encourage children to use context clues to determine the meaning of any unknown words. These strategies will help children learn to analyze the text more thoroughly as they read.

When you are finished reading this book, turn to the next-to-last page for **Text-Dependent Questions** and an **Extension Activity**.

TABLE OF CONTENTS

CONNECTED TO THE WORLD

Do you like to solve puzzles? Would you enjoy writing a set of instructions in a secret coded language? That is what it feels like to work in internet technology. Engineers, designers, and technicians work on the internet. But, what is the internet?

The internet is texting your friends to say how your day is going. It's posting news about yourself on Facebook and reading news posted by other people.

To prepare for a job in internet technology, you'll need to study science, technology, engineering, art, and math.

It's playing a YouTube video on your tablet. It's running a game on your laptop that lets you compete **remotely** with other players. It's streaming a movie on your TV. It's browsing research on a computer to help you write a report for school.

How can the internet be all of these things?

STEAM Fast Fact:

No one knows for sure, but there are probably close to two billion websites. That's according to Internet Live Stats, a company that uses internet robots to ping every website and test whether it's active.

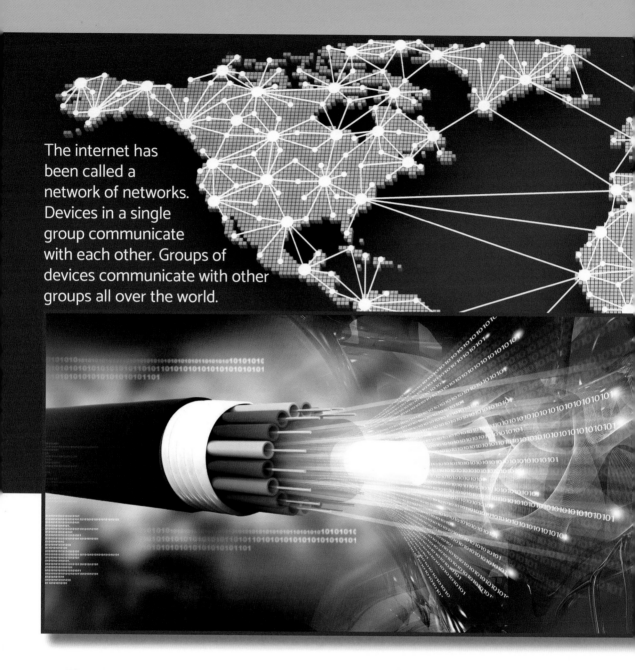

The internet has been called a network of networks. Devices in a single group communicate with each other. Groups of devices communicate with other groups all over the world.

The internet is a communications network that lets computers and other devices share information with each other electronically. The computers and devices send wireless signals through the air or send signals of light through a worldwide system of fiber-optic cables.

When you use the internet, you are connected to people, businesses, news, and research everywhere. That's a powerful thing!

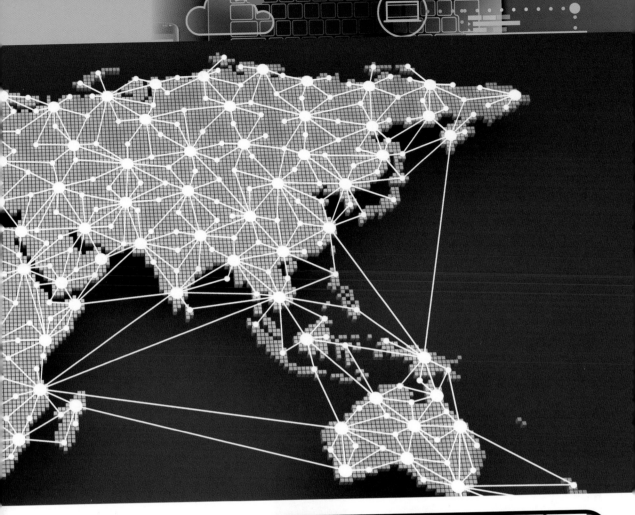

Real STEAM Job:
Web Developer

A web developer creates the layout of a site and determines how it will function. Will it post news? Let you shop for products? Link you to other websites? Web developers talk to

clients about their needs. They design visually attractive pages and write the code that makes the site function in a user-friendly way. Web developers rely on skills in art, math, and computer science.

STEAM Spotlight

How can you tell whether a site is a web page or an app? Most Internet websites are **static** pages that function just like a poster or a document you can read. But other websites are actually apps delivered to you through your web browser. One giveaway that you're using an app instead of a simple web page is the level of interactivity.

For example, Netflix and Kindle function like software—they're something you use, instead of just look at. Facebook and Google Maps are other examples of websites that are actually apps.

Real STEAM Job: Search Engine Optimization Specialist

A search engine optimization specialist (SEO specialist) understands how to design websites that will be found quickly and easily by search engines. These professionals are good problem-solvers and decision makers.

SEO specialists know how to place key words and phrases so that websites will be the first ones that users find and click on. They optimize—or maximize—a website's usefulness and popularity. These technology workers must understand computer science, human psychology, and language arts.

BUILDING THE INTERNET

The internet delivers text, pictures, and videos **intact** from one computer to another one miles away. How does it do that so reliably? One answer is that information has many possible ways to get where it needs to go. One of the earliest problems internet engineers worked on was how to get messages to arrive somewhere else by taking more than one route.

The U.S. Department of Defense (DOD) was the driving force behind an early version of the internet called the Advanced Research Projects Agency Network (ARPANET). The DOD in the 1950s wanted a communications system that would still work if parts of it were damaged by an enemy attack.

Real STEAM Job: Systems Programmer

A systems programmer is a high-level computer programmer who works with large networks of computers to maintain and control system software.

These professionals understand the big picture of how the internet works and write software code that helps different kinds of computers talk to each other. A systems programmer must have strong computer science and engineering skills.

Engineers designed the internet as a web of cables connected at hubs known as **routers**. If one route was damaged or clogged with traffic, data went in a different direction.

Smart network routers at hubs are like traffic cops. They control the direction data flows on the internet.

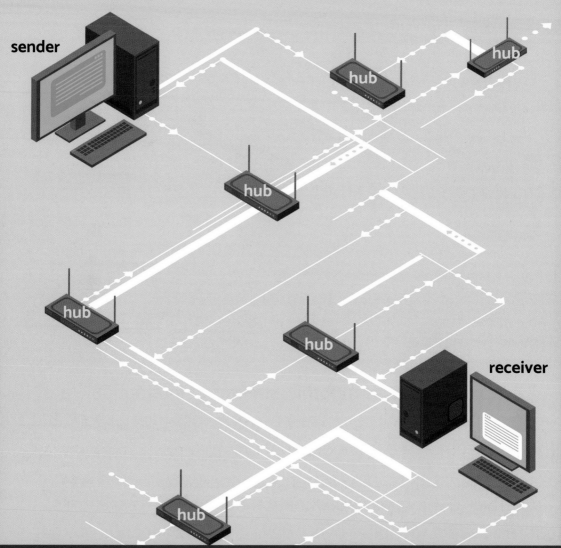

sender

receiver

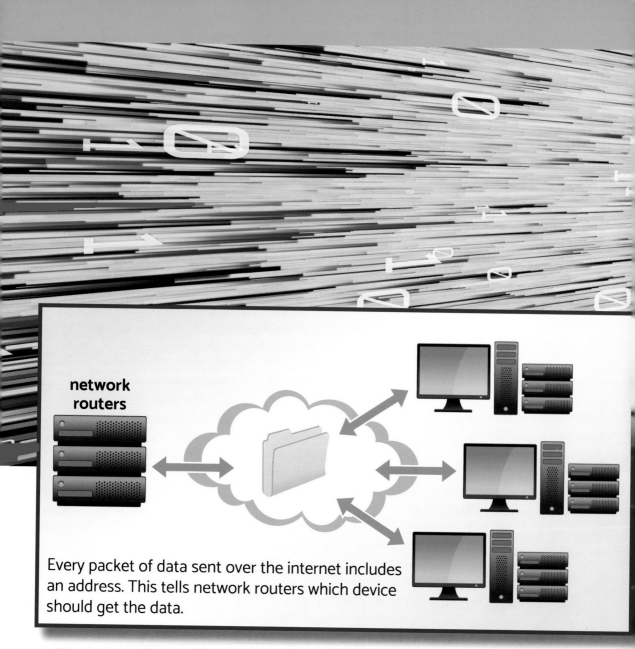

network
routers

Every packet of data sent over the internet includes an address. This tells network routers which device should get the data.

To move the traffic smoothly, streams of internet data are broken into small packets. They travel across the network and are then reassembled at their destination.

Getting to the correct destination depends on a system of addresses that identifies every device. It also depends on the network routers steering the packets in the proper direction. The result is a system that is very reliable, and very fast.

Real STEAM Job:
Network Architect

Internet traffic is growing every day. Network architects connect computers within a local network to each other, and externally to the internet. They monitor traffic from servers to make sure the system's equipment can handle the traffic with no downtime. They keep information from being lost by making backup copies and by installing software that protects computers against **cyberattacks** from outside the local area.

STEAM Spotlight

Your smartphone is so small. How can it store all of your videos, song files, and social media posts? It doesn't.

The data that appears on your phone is stored at different locations. Some is on your device, but much of it is on other very large computers called servers. It is retrieved when you need it by traveling across the internet. Keeping information, applications, and other computer services in different places is called storing it in the cloud.

Your data is in the cloud. What does that mean? In cloud computing, data is house far away on servers across the network. It gets delivered to you when you need it.

STEAM Fast Fact:

One of the earliest internet applications was electronic mail, or email. American computer programmer Ray Tomlinson is credited with the invention of email in 1972.

The *at* symbol is part of every email address. It goes in between the name of the person sending the email and the service used to transmit it.

A PLACE TO SHOP, SHARE, AND COLLABORATE

Before the internet, computers were mainly used to perform complex calculations. After the internet was developed, people realized computers could also be used to communicate.

ENIAC (electronic numerical integrator and computer) was the first large-scale computer to run at electronic speed. It was built between 1943 and 1945 and was used to perform complex calculations for the military.

Then in the 1990s and 2000s, new internet applications were invented that changed how people shopped, shared ideas, and worked together. You could buy products at Amazon, participate in an auction through eBay, download music at iTunes, and pay vendors online using PayPal.

When social media arrived, regular people could easily post information on the internet. They could stay in touch with friends on Facebook, send quick news updates on Twitter, and pin notes on Pinterest.

Mobile phones with internet access developed during this time too. Online applications showed up on these new smartphones as apps. Sharing, collaborating, and buying on the internet became widespread.

Real STEAM Job: IT Manager

Who are the people who imagine all of the ways we use the internet? One professional who plays a large role is the IT (information technology) manager. An IT manager thinks about how technology can be used to solve real-world problems. People in this role design a plan and lead a team of programmers, designers, and technicians in carrying it out. IT managers are in charge of coordinating and directing large computing networks that serve businesses and other organizations.

STEAM Spotlight

Someday, the internet may be used to track all the things people buy and sell. An internet-based system could replace banks and even paper money.

Already, some people use bitcoin to buy and sell items online. Bitcoin is a type of virtual coin. Trades in bitcoin are tracked on an internet-based ledger. That way, everyone knows how much bitcoin they have in their virtual wallets.

The ledger is powered by a technology called *blockchain*. It keeps an encrypted record of the value of everything that is bought and sold. It stores the records on all the computers on the network, so no one can cheat. People who design virtual ledgers like bitcoin's ledger are called *blockchain developers*.

HOW DOES
BLOCKCHAIN
WORK?

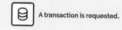 A transaction is requested.

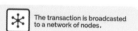 The transaction is broadcasted to a network of nodes.

 The network validates the transaction using known algorithms.

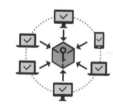

VALIDATION MAY INCLUDE

 SMART CONTRACTS

 CRYPTOCURRENCY

 OTHER RECORDS

 The transaction is unified with other transactions as a block of data.

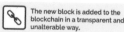 The new block is added to the blockchain in a transparent and unalterable way.

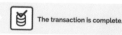 The transaction is complete.

BENEFITS OF THE BLOCKCHAIN

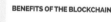 TRANSPARENCY AND TRA

 SIMPLER AND FASTER

 REDUCED COSTS

 INCREASED TRUST

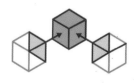

Real STEAM Job: Blockchain Developer

Expertise in blockchain is one of the most in-demand skills in the job market today. Blockchain developers use computer commands to design smart contracts, which are also known as ledgers. A smart contract is a series of instructions that cascade from one group of code to the next, until the people using the system reach the end of the contract. To become a blockchain developer, you'll need to be an experienced computer programmer with specialized knowledge about ledgers and how they work.

BLOCKCHAIN TECHNOLOGY USES

DIGITAL CURRENCY

FINANCE

IOT

DATA STORAGE

GOVERNANCE

ONLINE VOTING

HEALTH CARE

INSURANCE

PREDICTING THE FUTURE WITH BIG DATA

What if you could collect all of the information that's on the internet and use it to help you solve problems, or even predict people's behavior? That's what data scientists do.

Ever since personal computers became popular decades ago, people have been sending information across the internet. Now, internet servers have huge amounts of stored data.

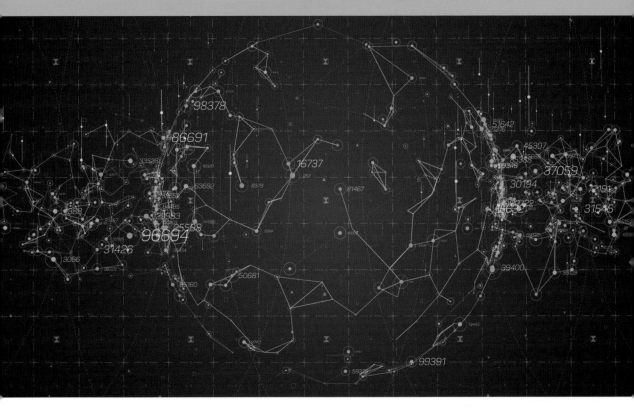

Asking the right questions is one key to using the vast amount of data stored on the internet.

The data on the internet is random in structure and is changing quickly every day. All the information together is called *big data*– and trying to sort through all of it to find out what the internet knows can be very complicated.

Data professionals draw large amounts of data from across many different places on the internet. They design computer **algorithms** that find patterns and detect trends in the data and in the behavior of people who surf the internet. They use that information to guess what's coming next.

Real STEAM Job: Database Manager

A database manager understands what data a company is collecting and storing and how it is organized in databases. This tech professional knows how to build and manage databases for different purposes. He or she directs a team of data professionals.

STEAM Spotlight

Amazon uses big data to track your shopping habits and create pop-up ads next to your purchases. The recommendations account for 35 percent of the company's sales.

Netflix uses big data to decide which TV shows and movies you might be interested in. Its recommendations guide 80 percent of the content we watch on Netflix.

President Obama's 2012 campaign used big data to find people who were likely to change their minds about who to vote for. Workers sent email and phone advertisements to these people. The strategy was key in helping the president win re-election.

In 2014 the Centers for Disease Control (CDC) and World Health Organization (WHO) used big data to predict the spread of an Ebola outbreak in West Africa. Big data helped the organizations decide where to set up medical centers and how to treat the disease.

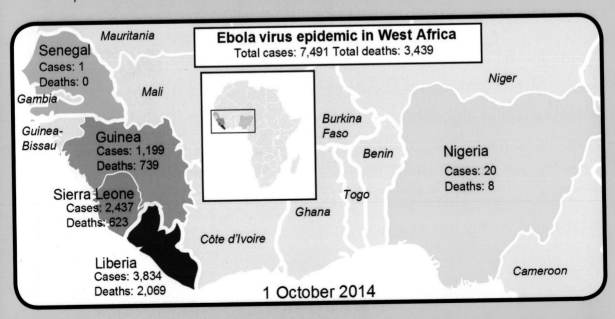

Ebola virus epidemic in West Africa
Total cases: 7,491 Total deaths: 3,439

Mauritania

Senegal
Cases: 1
Deaths: 0

Niger

Gambia

Mali

Guinea-Bissau

Guinea
Cases: 1,199
Deaths: 739

Burkina Faso

Benin

Nigeria
Cases: 20
Deaths: 8

Sierra Leone
Cases: 2,437
Deaths: 623

Togo

Ghana

Côte d'Ivoire

Liberia
Cases: 3,834
Deaths: 2,069

Cameroon

1 October 2014

Real STEAM Job: Data Scientist

Mining for information on the internet is not a straightforward task. Data scientists find and organize relevant data from the internet, build algorithms to analyze the data, and test their models to make sure they work. A data scientist must also be able to understand the business problems that companies are trying to solve. These professionals must have strong skills in math and computer science.

STEAM Fast Fact:

Using big data, Walmart found that sales of strawberry Pop Tarts increased sevenfold when a hurricane was forecasted. The company concluded that people stock up on nonperishable and comfort foods when they prepare for natural disasters.

STOPPING INTERNET ATTACKS

During the 2016 United States presidential election, internet **hackers** stole and released embarrassing emails written by leaders of the Democratic Party. Many people believed Russia was behind the attack. Because of the hack, some people doubted the election outcome when the Democratic nominee, Hillary Clinton, lost to Donald Trump.

From election tampering to freezing a consumer website, stealing personal records, shutting down an electric grid, or holding a company's network for ransom, cybercrime is a problem that costs the global economy about 500 million dollars annually.

Russian hackers sent Hillary Clinton's campaign chairman a fake email that looked like it was from Google. It asked him to change his password.

Real STEAM Job: Cybersecurity Analyst

Cyberattacks are on the rise worldwide, and companies pay
people well to protect them against the threat. Cybersecurity
analysts **implement** security measures on a network. They
anticipate security breaches by staying updated on evolving
hacker methods. They research new technologies that protect
networks from attacks. To be a cybersecurity analyst, it is helpful
to study computer science as well as criminal justice.

Companies hire cybersecurity analysts to combat cyberattacks. They fight hackers by breaking into systems themselves and then fixing the weaknesses they uncover.

There's a severe shortage of cybersecurity experts. By 2021, it's estimated that there will be three and a half million unfilled positions worldwide.

Real STEAM Job: Vulnerability Analyst

A vulnerability analyst is an IT professional who tries to think like a hacker. He or she locates the weak spots, or vulnerabilities, in a computer system so that they can be made stronger against attack. These sleuths must be excellent investigators, problem-solvers, and computer scientists.

STEAM Fast Fact:

Would you like to learn how a computer hacker thinks? A website called *Hacker Highschool* publishes lessons that help young people learn problem-solving techniques used in computer hacking. The site's creators hope that developing real-world cybersecurity skills will encourage more teens to choose cybersecurity careers.

A cybercrime happens when an attack is launched from one computer against another. There are two main reasons cybercriminals do this: to cause mischief, and to get money.

One example of an attack is WannaCry. In 2017, this cyberattack **scrambled** data on more than 200,000 computers in more than 150 countries. Many victims paid ransoms to unlock the data on their computers.

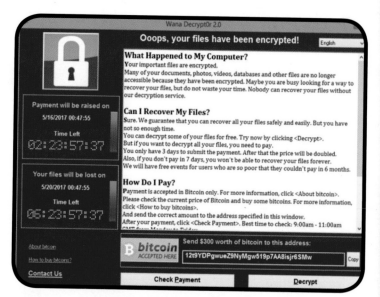

Victims of the WannaCry attack found their screens overtaken by a request for money.

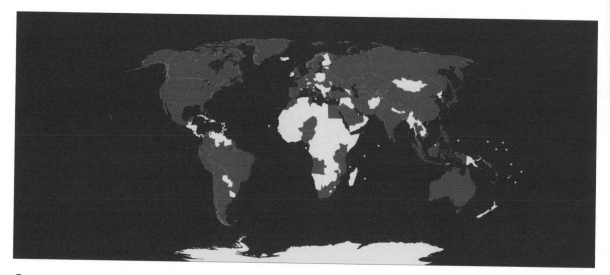

Countries shown in red were affected by the WannaCry cyberattack.

STEAM Spotlight

Most cybercrime relies on impersonation. Attackers fool a computer into believing they are someone it trusts. That's how an attack on the Ukraine power grid began. In 2015, hackers stole login names and passwords that allowed them to impersonate legitimate users. Once inside the network, they shut down several power substations. The attack turned off electricity for 230,000 residents.

THE INTERNET OF THINGS

Things around us are getting smarter. You can control your home's thermostat or lights with your smartphone. A fitness watch can monitor how much you exercise. A GPS tracker on your pet's collar can help you find its location.

Your dog just got smarter! Using IoT, your pet's collar can send information to your smartphone showing where your pooch has been.

The internet originally provided information to people. Now, the internet is also being used to provide information to things. This approach is called the internet of things, or IoT.

Engineers who design smart devices can connect any object with a **microchip** embedded in it to the internet. From there, it can interact with apps in the cloud or with other devices.

A microchip is the "thinking" part of an electronic device. It can sense what's around it, make a decision, and send instructions.

STEAM Spotlight

In cities such as San Francisco and Seattle, you can use an app to find a parking space. Sensors mounted on parking meters detect when a space is taken up by a vehicle and when it is available. The information is transmitted wirelessly to an internet cloud service, where anyone with a smartphone can access it.

Real STEAM Job: Wearable Tech Designer

These high-tech product developers use their wildest imaginations to design computers you can wear and take with you. They invent ways to incorporate microchips into watches, eyeglasses, luggage, shoes, and more.

Wearable computers might be used to send and receive messages or to collect data about location, activity levels, health status, and other important details. Tech designers need strong skills in computer science as well as in art and visual design.

STEAM Fast Fact:

According to IBM, trillions of sensors in our world monitor activities, track movement, and communicate with each other. Together, they populate the internet of things with real-time data.

STEAM Spotlight

In 2017, a company called Project Wing ran a drone test flight that delivered burritos and medicine to customers who ordered them on a mobile app.

Within a few years, it's expected there will be thousands of delivery drones in the sky at the same time. Project Wing is developing software that uses Google Maps and Google's cloud computing to help drones navigate millions of routes and process flight decisions in fractions of a second.

What do drones have to do with STEAM? Imagine you are working on developing some new package-delivery drones. You might ask yourself these questions.

Science: How will the drones be affected by wind and rain?
Technology: What computer components will the drones need to have?
Engineering: How will the parts fit together so the drones stay balanced?
Art: What will the drones look like? Will people like to look at them flying in the sky?
Math: How heavy can the packages be?

STEAM Spotlight

The internet can help farmers grow more crops. Sensors mounted in fields can monitor light, humidity, temperature, and soil moisture. The information is sent to a web-based service that automatically controls irrigation.

Real STEAM Job: Software Engineer

How do all the things connected to the internet become so smart? Each one is driven by software. Software is a set of coded instructions that tells computers and other devices what to do when commands are sent to it. The person who writes the coded instructions is a software engineer. Software engineers study computer languages and computer science.

Do you have some ideas about what aspects of the internet you would like to learn more about? Chances are, the job you have someday will relate to the global network that powers our world with information and connectivity. Developing STEAM skills will help you reach your goals.

STEAM JOB FACTS

Web Developer

Important Skills: creativity, logical thinking, ability to communicate with clients

Important Knowledge: visual design, coding languages, understanding of business needs

College Major: computer science, computer programming, visual art

Network Architect

Important Skills: attention to detail, troubleshooting problems, training people to use the network

Important Knowledge: math, computers, electronics, how to service equipment

College Major: computer science, computer engineering, information systems

Blockchain Developer

Important Skills: strong analytical abilities, good communicator

Important Knowledge: programming languages, code breaking, distributed computing

College Major: information security, computer science, software engineering

Data Scientist

Important Skills: strong analytical abilities, complex problem-solving abilities

Important Knowledge: statistics, programming languages, algorithm design

College Major: statistics, mathematics, economics, computer science, data science

Cybersecurity Analyst

Important Skills: deductive reasoning, troubleshooting for weaknesses, ability to research solutions

Important Knowledge: security technologies, software installation

College Major: computer science, computer engineering, criminal justice

Software Engineer

Important Skills: analytical thinking, good problem-solving abilities, teamwork

Important Knowledge: math, programming languages

College Major: computer science, computer engineering

GLOSSARY

algorithms (AL-guh-ri-thuhms): sets of steps that are followed in order to solve a mathematical problem or to complete a computer process

cyberattacks (SYE-bur-uh-taks): attempts to gain illegal access to a computer or computer system for the purpose of causing damage or harm

hackers (HAK-urs): people who have special skills for getting into computer systems without permission

implement (IM-pluh-ment): to put a plan or an idea into action

intact (in-TAKT): not broken or damaged

microchip (MYE-kroh-chip): a very thin piece of silicon that contains electronic circuits, used in computers and other electronic equipment

remotely (ri-MOHT-lee): from a distance

routers (rou-TURS): devices that handle signals between computers or computer networks

scrambled (SKRAM-buhld): altered an electronic signal so that it requires a special receiver to decode the message

static (STA-tik): not moving, changing, or growing

INDEX

TEXT-DEPENDENT QUESTIONS

1. What kind of functions can a web developer add to a web page?
2. How do the packets of data traveling across the internet get to the correct destination?
3. Where is the data in the cloud actually stored?
4. What is bitcoin?
5. What is one tactic cybercriminals use to break into someone else's computer?

EXTENSION ACTIVITY

Create a secret message to a friend by talking like a computer. Computers communicate by passing electronic signals back and forth. The signals work like a light switch: one for on, and zero for off. How can you talk with only ones and zeros? Use a lot of them! Go to www.elon.edu and search *codebreakers* to learn more about ASCII, a code that uses only ones and zeros. It will show you the combinations of ones and zeros that computers use to write each letter of the alphabet.

ABOUT THE AUTHOR

Carole Hawkins watched a computer spit out hundreds of coded punch cards at her dad's office at IBM when she was six years old. Today, she's a freelance journalist and former computer programmer who's still fascinated by how people get machines to think.

www.rourkeeducationalmedia.com

PHOTO CREDITS: Cover art © Andrey Suslov; Pages 4-5: Girl by locker © Monkey Business Images, STEAM illustration © Angela Matthews, computer and notepad © Diego Cervo; Pages 6-7 World Map © Vlad Kochelaevskiy, fiber optic cables © bluebay, Web Developer © Rawpixel.com; Pages 8-9 computer with SEO info © ilkercelik, Netflix Editorial credit: sitthiphong / Shutterstock.com, Phone with apps Editorial credit: BigTunaOnline / Shutterstock.com; Page 10 © FlashMovie; Pages 12-13 © yongheng19962008, computer network © Daryn Cox, woman © Mark Agnor; Page 14 Editorial credit: Studio Monkey / Shutterstock.com, cloud computing illustration © Jozsef Bagota, Page 15 © Kaspars Grinvalds; Page 17 Editorial credit: Evan Lorne / Shutterstock.com; Pages 18-19 Editorial credit: fyv6561 / Shutterstock.com, girl on computer Editorial credit: ximgs / Shutterstock.com, page 19 © fizkes; Pages 20-21 world map © naulicrea, Bitcoin © Visual Generation, chart © elenabsl; Pages 22-23 and 24-25 © metamorworks, code © BEST-BACKGROUNDS; Pages 26-27 Amazon photo Editorial credit: Worawee Meepian / Shutterstock.com, Netflix Editorial credit: dennizn / Shutterstock.com, Obama campaign website Editorial credit: Juan Camilo Bernal / Shutterstock.com; Page 28 © a-image, Page 29 Walmart store Editorial credit: Ken Wolter / Shutterstock.com, Pop tarts Editorial credit: dcwcreations / Shutterstock.com; Page 30 © BeeBright, Page 31 © Gorodenkoff; Page 32 © Gorodenkof, Page 33 © LightField Studios; Page 35 power grid © Vadven; Pages 36-37 holding ce phone © Andrey Suslov, dog and GPS tracker © Jelena Safronova, microchip © Victor Moussa; Page 38 © Tero Vesalainen, Page 39 By a-image; Pages 40-41 © NH; Page 42 © Lamyai, Page 43 © Pressmaster. All images from Shutterstock.com except page 11 ARPANET timeline © MichelBakni https://creativecommons.org/licenses/by-sa/4.0/deed.en; Page 16 courtesy of the U.S. Military; Pages 26-27 Map of Ebola virus in Africa public domain image © Mikael Häggström. Also updated © BrianGroen.; Page 34 map © TheAwesomeHwyh https://creativecommons.org/licenses/by-sa/3.0/deed.en, screen shot public domain image

Edited by: Kim Thompson
Produced by Blue Door Education for Rourke Educational Media. Cover and interior design by: Nicola Stratford

Library of Congress PCN Data

STEAM Jobs in Internet Technology / Carole Hawkins
(STEAM Jobs You'll Love)
ISBN 978-1-73161-477-3 (hard cover)
ISBN 978-1-73161-284-7 (soft cover)
ISBN 978-1-73161-582-4 (e-Book)
ISBN 978-1-73161-687-6 (e-Pub)
Library of Congress Control Number: 2019932398

Rourke Educational Media
Printed in the United States of America,
North Mankato, Minnesota